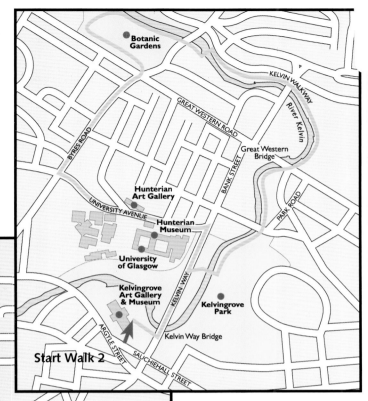

Start Walk 2

Street and enter the Italian Centre at the John Street entrance. Walk through the Italian courtyard and exit into Ingram Street. Turn left and pass Hutchesons' Hall and the Ramshorn Theatre on your way to the High Street. Turn left into the High Street and walk up to the **Cathedral precincts (pages 6–7)**. Visit Provand's Lordship, Glasgow's oldest house, the St Mungo Museum and medieval **Glasgow Cathedral (pages 8–9)**. A little extra time and energy is needed to reach the summit of the Necropolis but the city views are well worth the climb.

Return south along the High Street to **Glasgow Cross and Trongate (pages 10–11)**. If you have time, follow the

Trongate, into Argyle Street. Turn right into **Buchanan Street (pages 14–15)** to visit stylish Princes Square. Time permitting, visit The Lighthouse in Mitchell Lane. Then head north to turn left into **Sauchiehall Street** (for refreshments at the famous Willow Tea Rooms.

Walk up West: walk 2

Begin by exploring **Kelvingrove Art Gallery and Museum (pages 18–19)** at the top of Argyle Street. Exit the museum to the rear into Kelvingrove Park and turn left to cross the river at Kelvin Way Bridge. Follow **The Kelvin Way (pages 20–21)**, turning left into University Avenue, where you will find Glasgow University Visitor Centre, the Hunterian Museum and the Hunterian Art Gallery, including the reconstructed Mackintosh House.

Follow University Avenue, turning right into Byres Road. At the end of Byres Road, enter the Botanic Gardens. Exit at the steps to **The Kelvin (pages 22–23)** onto the Kelvin Walkway. Cross the iron bridge to the north bank and follow the river downstream to the Great Western Bridge. Follow the path under the bridge into Kelvingrove Park. Walk through the park to cross the Kelvin Way Bridge and return to Kelvingrove Art Gallery and Museum.

Welcome to Glasgow

Vibrant with art and music, colour and life, this dynamic European city is a thriving cultural and commercial centre. The regeneration of recent years has reshaped the centre with modern buildings complementing the eclectic mix of Georgian and Victorian buildings that defined the industrial wealth of Scotland's second capital. Enjoy some of the city treasures in the internationally acclaimed art galleries and museums, eat and drink in style in the many top-class restaurants, be entertained in world-famous venues or shop for designer clothes in the Merchant City. Take in the sights and sounds of Glasgow and your visit will be a truly memorable experience.

A short history

St Kentigern (also known as St Mungo) founded a monastery here in the 7th century. Kentigern was a Bishop of Strathclyde and, after his death, the site became a place of pilgrimage. A settlement grew up around Kentigern's shrine; in 1136 a cathedral was consecrated. Glasgow was granted a weekly market and an annual fair, establishing it as a major centre of trade. The town developed south of the cathedral and the pattern of the medieval streets can still be seen today, winding from Glasgow Cross uphill to Castle Street, where the bishop held court.

The 15th century saw a university established and Glasgow became a royal burgh in 1611. A great fire in 1652 destroyed one third of Glasgow's buildings – the flames rapidly consuming wooden walls and thatched roofs. After this, all new buildings were constructed from stone and slate. The 18th century saw the greatest expansion, when Glasgow became the leading port for tobacco imports from the Americas. The city expanded westwards as the wealthy 'Tobacco Lords' built their mansion houses away from the squalor of the centre. The Merchant City prospered, and by the time of the Industrial Revolution, Glasgow was the empire's second city. The River Clyde was deepened to allow ships to sail to a new dock at the Broomielaw. By 1870, more than half of Britain's shipbuilding workforce was based on the Clyde. New city developments throughout the 19th century employed the talents of architects such as Alexander Thomson and the innovative Charles Rennie Mackintosh, who designed some of the wonderful buildings that can be seen in Glasgow today.

The middle decades of the 20th century saw a decline in the traditional industries and, in the 1970s, the city began a regeneration project, landscaping derelict spaces, refurbishing old buildings and creating a stunning newwaterfront development. Glasgow wasEuropean City of Culture in 1990, European Capital of Sport in 2003 and will host the 2014 Commonwealth Games.

Glasgow Science Centre

Merchant City

The development of the Merchant City began in the 18th century as the prosperous merchants, known as the Tobacco Lords, began building their mansions to the west of the High Street, historically the backbone of the city. Lavish homes designed in the classical style were built on wide, straight streets with vistas and squares. This marked the beginning of a movement westward that would continue throughout the 19th century to the present day.

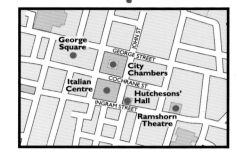

George Square

First laid out in 1781, George Square is the venue for celebrations, parades and meetings, and a number of historic political rallies and protests have been held here. Around the square are statues of people associated with the city, including equestrian statues of Queen Victoria and Prince Albert. The tall column in the centre supports a statue of Sir Walter Scott. The city cenotaph is on the east side of the square.

City Chambers

The City Chambers, on the east side of George Square, were opened in 1888 by Queen Victoria. This imposing building was created in an extravagant baroque style and the carved reliefs and statues celebrate the achievements of the British Empire. The magnificent interior, with its ornate ceilings, marble columns and staircases, and elaborate stained glass, includes many fine works of art. Guided tours are available during weekdays and are free of charge.

City Chambers

Italian Centre

Italian Centre

Opened in 1991, this stylish shopping arcade in John Street is based on an Italian palazzo, with residential flats, cafés, retail outlets and offices grouped around a central courtyard. Find exclusive boutiques, famous names, some unusual sculptures and a cup of real Italian coffee here.

Sculpture,
Italian Centre

Ramshorn Theatre

At the junction of Ingram Street and Candleriggs, the Ramshorn Theatre is housed in the converted neo-Gothic St David's Kirk, also known as Ramshorn Kirk, which was built in 1824 to replace an older building. The small but interesting graveyard contains the ornate tombs of many notable citizens. Student and community productions are presented here throughout the year and a permanent display of theatre photography can be seen in the theatre bar.

Ramshorn Theatre

The tower, Hutchesons' Hall

Hutchesons' Hall

Designed by David Hamilton and built in 1802, Hutchesons' Hall is one of Glasgow's most elegant buildings. The statues of the Hutcheson brothers on the façade date from an earlier building of 1641. Inside, an imposing staircase leads up to the Grand Hall where regular exhibitions are held. The building is the west of Scotland headquarters of the National Trust for Scotland and a gallery selling work by young Glasgow designers is a source for some interesting and unusual gifts.

Cathedral precincts

The High Street is Glasgow's medieval thoroughfare, winding uphill from Glasgow Cross to Castle Street and the cathedral precincts, where the bishop had his castle and the canons their dwellings. This is the route the pilgrims took to the shrine of St Mungo, and the very heart of Glasgow life. In the 19th century, the High Street was rebuilt with the tenement buildings and shops we see today.

Provand's Lordship

On the west side of Castle Street is Provand's Lordship, Glasgow's oldest house, which was built in 1471 as part of St Nicholas's Hospital. Restored by the Provand's Lordship Society, this historical building offers a rare insight into the architecture of early Glasgow and depicts a 17th-century domestic interior.

Provand's Lordship from St Nicholas Physic Garden

St Nicholas Physic Garden

To the rear of Provand's Lordship, St Nicholas Physic Garden has been recreated to show plants in common use during the medieval period for medicinal purposes. There is a formal parterre garden at the centre. This haven of tranquillity recalls the role of the medieval hospital, founded by Bishop Muirhead in 1471, which once stood on the site.

Carving, St Nicholas Physic Garden

St Mungo Museum of Religious Life and Art

St Mungo Museum of Religious Life and Art

Created in period style and opened to the public in 1993, the St Mungo Museum of Religious Life and Art was designed to raise awareness of the importance of religion in people's lives throughout the world, and to promote a mutual understanding and respect across all faiths. Three permanent exhibition areas depict religious life and art, and there is also a temporary exhibition space. A café offers lunches and light refreshments.

Peaceful place

'Where We Are' is the name of Britain's first permanent Zen garden, created at the St Mungo Museum by Yasutaro Tanaka in the Japanese Zen Buddhist tradition. Only natural materials are used in the garden, which aims to inspire contemplation, tranquillity and peace.

Zen garden

Glasgow Necropolis

A short walk from the cathedral, the Glasgow Necropolis contains the remains of some of the most eminent Glaswegians. Wealthy families commissioned splendid monuments designed by the fashionable architects of the day including Alexander 'Greek' Thomson, David Hamilton and Charles Rennie Mackintosh. The best views of the cathedral can be seen from the summit and, on a clear day, you can see the Clyde valley and the hills of Cowal to the west.

Glasgow Necropolis

Glasgow Cathedral

Glasgow Cathedral is a rare example of Scottish medieval architecture and the only mainland cathedral in Scotland to have survived the Reformation almost intact. St Mungo established a church on this site at the beginning of the 7th century and was buried here in the year 612. Tales of his miracles drew pilgrims to the shrine and a cathedral was consecrated in 1136. This earlier building was destroyed in a fire. The present building's construction began in 1179 and continued throughout the 12th and 13th centuries, with later additions.

Upper church

Entering by the south door, the first impression is of space and light – the open timber roof, which dates from the 14th century, is 32 metres (105 feet) high. Separating the nave from the choir, the ornate choir screen or *pulpitum*, completed in the early 15th century, is an astonishing construction and displays the accomplished craft of the medieval master masons. The site of the church slopes from west to east, allowing the unusual construction of a lower church occupying the whole area beneath the choir.

The nave

Blackadder Aisle

The Blackadder Aisle is said to occupy the site of a cemetery consecrated by St Ninian at the beginning of the 5th century. Part of the lower church, it was built by Archbishop Blackadder around 1500. The striking white pillars rise to a vaulted roof decorated with unusual carvings known as vaulting bosses; these include the Blackadder arms. Originally intended as a crypt to a chapel above, the aisle is associated with the story of St Kentigern and may have played an important part in the pilgrims' route around the cathedral.

Lower church

Fragments of the original 12th-century building survive in the lower church. St Kentigern's tomb and part of the 13th-century shrine to the saint can still be seen in this remarkable feature of the cathedral with its decorated columns and high vaulted ceilings. A series of chapels at the east end includes the Chapel of St John the Evangelist containing St Kentigern's well.

Detail from the Millennium Window

Glorious glass

The cathedral contains some interesting examples of contemporary stained glass, including the window above the west door by Francis Spear (1958) and the beautiful blue Millennium Window in the north wall of the nave. This piece of work by John Clark, which was produced employing traditional techniques, is regarded as one of the finest examples of modern stained glass.

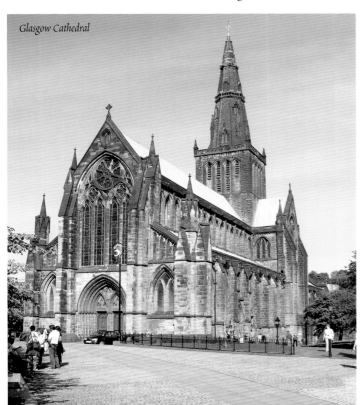

Glasgow Cathedral

Glasgow Cross and Trongate

High Street, London Road, Saltmarket, Gallowgate and Trongate all meet at Glasgow Cross, where the building of the burgh began and the first weekly markets were held in the 12th century. Glasgow Cross in the 1700s was the centre of trade and commerce. Here was the Tron to weigh goods coming into the town, the Tolbooth for civic matters, the prison and the gallows. A new town hall was erected in 1738 and buildings took on a distinctly Venetian style with arcaded streets and piazzas. Only the Tolbooth Steeple and the Tron Steeple survived the restructuring of Glasgow Cross in the 19th and 20th centuries.

Mercat Cross

The Mercat Cross seen today replaces a cross removed in 1659. Ceremoniously erected in 1930, it was built in the form of an octagonal tower with a heraldic unicorn forming the top of the cross. All over Scotland, crosses like this can still be seen marking places where markets were legally held. They were important meeting places and became the focal point for many town events.

Mercat Cross

Tolbooth Steeple

Tron Steeple

The Tron Steeple, built in the 1630s, is one of Glasgow's most recognised landmarks. A 15th-century church on the site was burned down by members of the Hellfire Club (a term loosely used to describe members of notorious drinking clubs) in 1793. In an act of drunken vandalism, a number of young men built up the open hearth until the contents of the fireplace spilled out onto the wooden floor setting alight the whole building. Only the steeple survived, incorporated into a new building designed by James Adam, presently the home of the Tron Theatre.

Tolbooth Steeple

Topped with a stone crown, the Tolbooth Steeple, standing seven storeys high, is all that remains of the old Tolbooth built by the town council in 1627. As Glasgow's council chamber, the building once housed the council hall, the town clerk's office and the city prison. Demolished after the First World War, the outline of the main structure can be seen on the west side of the tower.

Tron Steeple

Depiction of a Tobacco Lord, 1901

Scotland's first millionaires

The Tobacco Lords made vast sums of money by importing tobacco into Glasgow and re-exporting it into Europe. They became Scotland's first millionaires and invested their huge profits in trade, finance and industry, building fine mansion houses in the city and purchasing large country estates. This new elite dominated Glasgow socially and economically until the American Wars of Independence caused a collapse in the tobacco trade in the 1770s.

The Plainstanes

A new town hall built in the Trongate in 1740 faced a paved area known as the 'Plainstanes', which was reserved for the exclusive use of the famous Tobacco Lords. As one 18th-century writer described: 'No one dared to intrude upon their promenade ground. They strutted about on the Plainstanes as if they were the rulers of the destinies of Glasgow attired in scarlet cloaks, curled wigs, cocked hats, and bearing gold-headed canes.'

The Plainstanes in the 18th century

Glasgow Green and the People's Palace

Glasgow Green is the city's oldest park and for centuries it functioned as the only public open space. Granted to Bishop Turnbull by James II in 1450, and gifted by the bishop to the people of Glasgow for common grazing, it was also used for bleaching linen and drying fishing nets. The Green became a favourite meeting place and throughout the centuries witnessed many important events in the history of Glasgow. Within the park grounds is Glasgow's museum of social history, known as the People's Palace, with its beautiful glass-domed Winter Gardens.

The People's Palace

Standing at the centre of the park, this impressive sandstone and glass building houses a vast collection of Glasgow memorabilia. From a dug-out canoe of the 6th-century salmon fishers to the story of the great shipyards of the Clyde, the collection tells of the struggles and triumphs of the working people of Glasgow. Interactive displays include oral histories and archive film, prints, photographs, paintings and a wealth of artefacts that bring the history of ordinary Glaswegians to life.

Bonnie Prince Charlie

Smudge the cat

The most famous of the employees at the People's Palace was Smudge the cat. A mascot popular with staff and visitors, she featured in a number of campaigns including 'Paws off Glasgow Green' in 1990. Smudge was even a member of the General, Municipal and Boilermakers Union after NALGO refused her admission as a blue-collar worker.

Smudge ceramic by Margery Clinton

The thorn tree

After taking Glasgow in 1745, Bonnie Prince Charlie surveyed his troops on Glasgow Green. A thorn tree marking the spot where he stood became one of Glasgow's most popular sights. Souvenir hunters gradually reduced the tree to a stump and, in time, even that disappeared. Today, a new thorn tree has been planted, marked by Prince Charlie's Gate.

Doulton Fountain

City of Glasgow coat of arms, Doulton Fountain

Doulton Fountain

The largest terracotta fountain in the world, the Doulton Fountain is 14 metres (46 feet) high and 21 metres (70 feet) wide at its base. Presented to the city by manufacturers Doulton & Co, the fountain, decorated with Queen Victoria at the apex and groups of figures representing the colonies of the British Empire, was made for display at the Glasgow International Exhibition in 1888, held at Kelvingrove and moved to Glasgow Green in 1890.

Winter Gardens

Enjoy the café in the Winter Gardens with its open views across Glasgow Green. Attached to the People's Palace, this elegant glasshouse filled with palms, ferns and exotic plants offers a programme of exhibitions and events throughout the year. When it was first built in 1898, the Winter Gardens was a great glass auditorium staging regular musical performances. Open all year round, it is a warm and delightful retreat during the winter months.

Winter Gardens

Buchanan Street to Sauchiehall Street

Buchanan Street is the central axis of Glasgow, connecting the Glasgow Royal Concert Hall and the Buchanan Galleries at the eastern end of Sauchiehall Street with Argyle Street. This pedestrianized street with its attractive tree planting and comfortable seating areas was voted the third-best street in Britain. Traffic-free shopping continues into Sauchiehall Street, whose name is from the Scots for 'low-lying meadow with willows'.

Princes Square

Developed in 1987 from an existing four-storey merchant's court built in 1841, the exterior of the Princes Square shopping arcade in Buchanan Street is overlooked by a distinctive peacock sculpture. Glass-sided elevators, baroque staircases and escalators carry shoppers to five levels of specialist shops and boutiques. Here are fountains, mosaics and sculptures, and the fashionable bars and restaurants stay open until midnight.

Princes Square

Buskers, Sauchiehall Street

View from The Lighthouse

The Lighthouse

The Lighthouse was originally the *Glasgow Herald's* newspaper office, designed in 1895 by Charles Rennie Mackintosh. Today it is part of Architecture and Design Scotland, and has a range of changing exhibitions, events and activities. There are uninterrupted views over the city from the Mackintosh Tower, which is accessed by a helical staircase. A rooftop viewing platform at the south of the building can be accessed by a lift.

Buchanan Galleries

Making a bold statement at the north end of Buchanan Street is the modern shopping complex known as the Buchanan Galleries. Opened in 1998, the complex covers 55,742 square metres (600,000 square feet). The largest city centre retail scheme to be built in Scotland during the 1990s, it accommodates around 80 branches of well-known shopping chains.

Buchanan Street shoppers

The Willow Tea Rooms

The Willow Tea Rooms

Take tea Mackintosh-style at the Willow Tea Rooms, designed by Charles Rennie Mackintosh for Kate Cranston (see panel) in 1903. All the furniture, fixtures and fittings – and even the dresses of the original waitresses – were designed by Mackintosh. Several rooms were created in the Sauchiehall Street premises, including the famous and exclusive Salon de Luxe, with its beautiful leaded glasswork, silver-painted furniture, and silk and velvet upholstery. Customers would willingly pay an extra penny for a cup of tea here.

Kate Cranston

Kate Cranston (1849–1934)

Kate Cranston opened her first tea room in 1878. She went on to open three more, including the famous Willow Tea Rooms. The elegant surroundings and high standards of service at her establishments made them popular meeting places for well-to-do women. She was a patron of both Mackintosh and his wife, Margaret Macdonald, who contributed to the interior design of all her premises.

Glasgow Royal Concert Hall

A statue of Donald Dewar (1937–2000), the First Minister of Scotland in the Parliament of 1999, stands in front of the sweeping curves of the Royal Concert Hall at the junction between Buchanan Street and Sauchiehall Street. Opened in 1990, the hall has been widely praised for its fine acoustics. The main auditorium can seat 2,400 people. This prestigious music venue also houses conference facilities, bars and restaurants.

Beside The Clyde

The Tall Ship

The River Clyde is the setting for some of Glasgow's most famous waterfront sights, old and new. Here for all to enjoy are the Finnieston Crane, the Glasgow Science Centre, Glasgow Tower, the Tall Ship at Glasgow Harbour, the Clyde Auditorium, known affectionately as 'The Armadillo', and – spanning the river – the Millennium Bridge and Clyde Arc.

The Broomielaw

The Broomielaw was once a bustling quayside where cargoes unloaded close to the city centre. It was here in 1812 that Europe's first passenger steamboat service started for travel between Glagow and Greenock on the paddle steamer *Comet*, built by Scotsman Henry Bell. Paddle steamers also ferried their passengers 'doon the watter' for a week's holiday in the popular resorts of Dunoon and Ayr. Thousands of Scottish emigrants boarded clipper ships at the Broomielaw, bound for America, Australia and New Zealand.

The Tall Ship at Glasgow Harbour

The *Glenlee* is one of only five Clyde-built sailing ships still afloat. Built in Port Glasgow in 1896 as a cargo vessel, the *Glenlee* is a windjammer with a steel hull and characteristic square sails. A favourite for families to explore, the ship can also act as a venue for conferences and unusual birthday parties. All a far cry from the days when she rounded Cape Horne in a force 9 gale …. In 2011 the *Glenlee* is due to relocate from Glasgow Harbour to a new site alongside the Riverside Museum (see p28).

Finnieston Crane

Old meets new at this well-known landmark, preserved as a symbol of Glasgow's engineering heritage. Standing 59 metres (195 feet) high, the Finnieston Crane was built in 1932 to lift engines and other large engineering products onto ships for export from the Clyde. Spanning the river here is the Clyde Arc, a bridge built in 2006 with sleek modern lines – a gateway into the city from the Pacific Quay.

Finnieston Crane and the Clyde Arc

Glasgow Science Centre

This futuristic science and technology complex contains the Scottish Power Planetarium, three floors of interactive exhibits, Scotland's only IMAX cinema – which has a screen larger than a five-a-side football pitch – and the Glasgow Tower, which at 127 metres (417 feet) high, is the tallest freestanding structure in the world capable of rotating 360 degrees from its foundations. The views of the city and surrounding countryside from the top of the tower are breathtaking.

Glasgow Science Centre   *Glasgow Tower, the planetarium and IMAX cinema, Glasgow Science Centre*

Clyde Auditorium

Nicknamed 'The Armadillo', the inspiration for the design of this striking, curvaceous building in steel and glass was a series of ships' hulls, wholly in keeping with the heritage of its position on what was once Queen's Dock. One of the country's, and indeed Europe's, leading concert venues hosting acts from all over the world, it is part of the award-winning Scottish Exhibition and Conference Centre which has first-class facilities. Seen from the river, the Clyde Auditorium complements Glasgow Science Centre on the South Bank: the two buildings – visually connected by the graceful lines of the Millennium Bridge – create a beautiful and impressive futuristic skyline.

'The Armadillo'

Kelvingrove Art Gallery and Museum

After a three-year period of closure for major refurbishment, Kelvingrove Art Gallery and Museum opened its doors again in July 2006. Built in 1901 of red sandstone in a Spanish baroque style, the building stands at the edge of Kelvingrove Park on Argyle Street. Regarded as Glasgow's premier museum, Kelvingrove holds one of Europe's great civic art collections and is one of Scotland's most popular visitor attractions.

'Heads', Sophie Cave

Inspiration and enlightenment

Kelvingrove has been described as 'the future of museums'. Innovative presentations in 22 themed galleries showcase the 8,000 exhibits, which range from natural history to one of the finest collections of arms and armour in the world. Interactive displays and a mini museum encourage young children to join in with the hands-on fun.

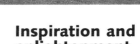

The foyer

The art galleries

The art collection is displayed in galleries designed to encourage a deeper understanding of the artists, their lives and work. Enjoy the canvasses of Monet, Pissaro and Matisse among the French Impressionists and Post-Impressionists, and the rich textures of the Dutch and Italian Masters. Discover the originality of the Glasgow Boys, who were influenced by social realism, and the four painters known as the Scottish Colourists. Throughout the corridors, sculptures and groups of paintings are placed strategically to utilise the architecture and vistas of this splendid building.

'Christ of St John of the Cross',
Salvador Dalí

The nation's favourite

Visitors from all over the world come to see Salvador Dali's *Christ of Saint John of the Cross*. The painting was acquired in 1952 by Dr Tom J. Honeyman, Director of Glasgow Museums, for the sum of £8,200. In 2005, a poll conducted by *The Herald* newspaper declared it to be Scotland's favourite painting.

Kelvingrove Art Gallery and Museum

'Return to Sender',
Sean Read

Festival organ

A magnificent organ was made for the Glasgow Festival of 1901. You can still hear the pipes echo around the staircases and galleries of this landmark building, as organ recitals are held regularly.

Sculptures

Sculptures can be seen on the main balconies and in prominent positions in alcoves and under arches. *Return to Sender*, a controversial impression of Elvis Presley by Sean Read, is a popular sculpture seen at the top of the west stairs on the ground floor. The recently restored *Motherless* by George Lawson, an old favourite, can be seen on the west balcony. Some sculptures have been placed appropriately, like *Robert Burns* by Kellock Brown outside the Scottish Gallery and *Madame Renoir* at the entrance to the French collection.

The Kelvin Way

Kelvingrove Park, with its famous view to Gilmorehill and the University Tower, lies behind the Kelvingrove Art Gallery and Museum. Enjoy the tree-lined stroll along the Kelvin Way, reached by crossing the red sandstone Kelvin Way Bridge with its impressive bronze sculptures, to the Gothic halls of Glasgow University and the Hunterian Museum.

Hunterian Museum

Scotland's oldest public museum, the Hunterian, opened in 1807. Home to a million items, this facinating museum has permanent displays of the history of medicine in Scotland, zoology, dinosaurs, coins and much more. The museum was originally the collection of William Hunter from East Kilbride, a distinguished physician who bequeathed 12,000 books, archeological and geological artefacts, and miscellaneous curiosities to Glasgow University in 1783.

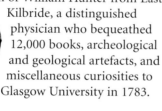

The University Tower from Kelvingrove Park

'Inspiration' statue, Kelvin Way Bridge

Glasgow University Visitor Centre

Founded in 1451, Glasgow is the second oldest university in Scotland. Located originally in the High Street, the university was relocated in 1870. Tours of the campus with its Gothic pinnacled buildings are available between April and September (booking is advisable). On certain days, the guided tour includes a climb to the top of the University Tower for some privileged views across Glasgow.

Kelvin Way Bridge

The single span of this red sandstone bridge carries the Kelvin Way over the River Kelvin. The four pairs of statues, regarded as some of the city's finest, represent war and peace, navigation and shipbuilding, philosophy and inspiration, and commerce and industry. Hit by a bomb during the Second World War, the statue most damaged was the one representing war. An arm from one of the statues – detached by the explosion – lay on the riverbed until it was spotted by a passer-by in 1995.

The Mackintosh House

The exterior of the Mackintosh House can be seen attached to the main building of the Hunterian Gallery. This remarkable reconstruction comprises the interiors created by Mackintosh and his wife, Margaret Macdonald, in their house at 78 Southpark Avenue. The couple lived there from 1906 to 1914 and made substantial alterations, removing walls and adding fixtures and fittings they had designed. The interiors include original Mackintosh furniture and a selection of soft furnishings based on contemporary descriptions of the house.

'Philosophy' statue, Kelvin Way Bridge

Drawing room, The Mackintosh House

Hunterian Art Gallery

The Hunterian Art Gallery houses a remarkable collection, including works by the Glasgow Boys and the Scottish Colourists. It also has the largest collection of Whistler paintings outside the USA. The Mackintosh Collection comprises over 800 drawings, designs and watercolours, featuring all aspects of the work of Charles Rennie Mackintosh, plus furnishings, letters and photographs.

Whistler paintings at the Hunterian Art Gallery

The Kelvin

The Kelvin Walkway follows the River Kelvin all the way through the west end of Glasgow, with access points at most bridges as well as steps up to surrounding city streets. Free from traffic, it extends for nine miles, starting in East Dunbartonshire and finishing on the north bank of the River Clyde at Glasgow Docks. The walkway includes access to the Botanic Gardens and offers a pleasant stroll along the riverside path back to Kelvingrove Art Gallery and Museum.

Glasgow Botanic Gardens

Glasgow Botanic Gardens

Recognized internationally for their impressive glasshouses and collections of plants from around the world, Glasgow Botanic Gardens are laid out with formal and themed plantings, a shady arboretum and peaceful riverside walks. Eleven linked glasshouses contain seasonal displays, carnivorous plants, tropical ferns and a tropical pond house with large water lilies. The orchid house is not to be missed, and an interesting collection in the tropical economic house cultivates examples of plants used for food, medicine, dyes, timber and clothes.

Kibble Palace statue

River Kelvin

Kibble Palace

Erected as a huge conservatory at the Loch Long home of engineer John Kibble, this unique glasshouse was leased from him by the Royal Botanic Institution of Glasgow in 1871. The structure was brought up the Clyde by barge, reconstructed, enlarged and opened as an exhibition and concert venue. In 1881, the palace was converted into a plant house for the cultivation of temperate plants, including a collection of Australian tree ferns still in residence after 120 years.

Kelvin riverbank

There are traces of old industries on the walk along the Kelvin riverbank, where the iron-rich water has been coloured by mine workings. Once mills ground flint to make glaze for pipes and tiles and, at Kelvinbridge, one of Glasgow's largest cotton mills was powered by the rushing weir built over the River Kelvin. Local birdlife includes heron, cormorant, kingfisher and mallard, and the river contains brown trout, salmon and sea trout. Fishing on the river is managed by the River Kelvin Angling Association and a permit can be obtained at most tackle shops in Glasgow.

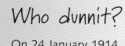

Kibble Palace

Who dunnit?

On 24 January 1914, 27 panes of glass from Kibble Palace were broken by a bomb allegedly planted by militant suffragettes. A second explosion was narrowly avoided when the burning end of a lighted fuse was cut off by the night stoker. Possible evidence that it was the work of suffragettes included the impression of high-heeled shoes in the soft ground and a lady's black silk scarf found nearby ....

In the 'Glasgow Style'

Those familiar with the work of Charles Rennie Mackintosh will be familiar with the Glasgow Style. The distinctive decorative forms, the ingenious architecture and stunning interiors are a part of the Glasgow landscape. Mackintosh was not alone in this new movement fostered by the progressive Glasgow School of Art in the 1880s, but his genius influenced a generation of young designers and he will always be regarded as the father of the Glasgow Style.

Glasgow Rose

A very popular motif was the 'Glasgow Rose', which was adapted from a design by Aubrey Beardsley and employed widely within Glasgow Style design. Influences for the Glasgow Style came from the Arts and Crafts Movement, art nouveau, Celtic imagery and the enlightened leadership of Francis Newbery, who introduced pottery, metalwork, stained glass and woodcarving to the Glasgow School of Art.

Glasgow School of Art

Glasgow School of Art

At the centre of this progressive movement was the Glasgow School of Art under the enlightened direction of the principal, Francis Newbery. He made connections with local manufacturers and encouraged the development of a technical studio, enabling students to master a range of crafts including metalwork and stained glass. Saturday morning and evening classes encouraged attendance from a wide variety of professions; Mackintosh first attended evening classes at the art school to complement his work as an apprentice architect.

THE GLASGOW SCHOOL OF ART 167

Francis Newbery (1855–1946)

The principal of the Glasgow School of Art between 1885 and 1918, Francis Newbery worked tirelessly to develop a prestigious modern art school for Glasgow. He was a staunch supporter of Mackintosh and a close friend throughout his life. Newbery's vision and encouragement contributed to the success of many well-known Glasgow artists.

Charles Rennie Mackintosh

'The Four'

Mackintosh married Margaret Macdonald, a kindred spirit he first met at the art school. Together with their mutual friend Herbert McNair and Margaret's sister, Jessie, they became known as 'The Four'. As a team they created innovative graphics, furniture and decorative art designs in beaten metalwork and silver. In 1896, they exhibited at the Arts and Crafts Exhibition in London, promoting the development and recognition of the distinctive 'Glasgow Style'.

The library, Glasgow School of Art

Where to see the Glasgow Style

Make your own tour of the Glasgow Style, looking at buildings, furnishings, paintings and interiors associated with the movement. Begin in the city centre, visiting the art school and enjoying a room devoted to the Glasgow Style at the Kelvingrove Art Gallery and Museum. The Hunterian Gallery holds a collection of artworks by some of the major players, including all members of 'The Four'. There are guided tours available and the Charles Rennie Mackintosh Society offers special tours including accommodation and transport.

Glasgow past and present

The early 19th century saw a huge growth in the population of Glasgow. The age of the entrepreneurs introduced new manufacturing industries, and the Clyde was developed as a port and a centre for shipbuilding. The city buildings tell the story – from the grand architecture boasting empire and wealth to the hidden closes of the city's east end where over-crowding and poverty were once commonplace. Today, many of the grand buildings have been developed into shops, restaurants, galleries and theatres and new housing developments have replaced some of the old tenements. Where warehouses once bustled with the commerce of the River Clyde, bright new offices stand as testament to the innovative ideas of Glasgow's young architects.

Tenement House

Tenements on the High Street

Tenement House

At 145 Buccleuch Street, a five-minute walk from Sauchiehall Street, the National Trust for Scotland has preserved this time capsule, the former home of Miss Agnes Toward, a shorthand typist, who first moved here in 1911. Victorian furniture, household bills, recipes, photographs and newspaper cuttings are examples of the paraphernalia of everyday living preserved by Agnes during her life. All the original fixtures and fittings can still be seen, including the kitchen box-beds and the old black-leaded range, once at the very heart of domestic life in the tenement flats.

Gallery of Modern Art

Gallery of Modern Art

Housed in the elegant Royal Exchange building, the Gallery of Modern Art was opened in 1996. The building dates from 1778 and was originally the town house of William Cunninghame, a wealthy Tobacco Lord. It was remodelled in the early 19th century for the Royal Exchange. The modern interiors reflect the elements – Earth, Water, Fire and Air – and include galleries of contemporary work. Among the exhibits are paintings and sculptures from around the world and works by renowned Scottish artists such as John Bellany and Ken Currie.

Tenement life

During the industrial expansion of the first half of the 19th century, workers left their traditional rural occupations to come to Glasgow, seeking a better life working in the factories and the heavy engineering industries. The tenement was an ideal way of housing a population that grew rapidly, providing accommodation to suit the incomes of different social classes. In working-class areas, tenement flats had only one or two rooms, and one-room flats, referred to as 'single ends', often accommodated a large family.

Barrowland market sign, on display at the People's Palace

The Barras

In the 19th century, street traders, trading from barrows, worked all over Glasgow, selling all manner of goods to supply the working people with their daily necessities. The huge increase in street trading following the First World War forced the city corporation to introduce measures to limit the number of barrows. James and Maggie McIver, who owned a barrow hire business, responded by organising a weekly market in Moncur Street known as Barrowland. This famous market, open at weekends, is affectionately known as 'The Barras'.

The Barras in the early 20th century

Around the Glasgow area

Glasgow has one of the finest public transport systems in Europe. The city train and bus systems operate frequent services and there are special day tickets available making the many attractions beyond the city centre easy to access. There are park and ride facilities throughout the city.

Transport exhibits

Transport museum

Following a major project, what was the Museum of Transport is due to reopen in 2011 at its new site at the Riverside Museum, where the Rivers Kelvin and Clyde meet. Interactive displays, 'toys for the boys' and, of course, much nostalgia will be here, along with changing exhibits: trains and trams, collections of vintage cars and horse-drawn vehicles, the original models of ships built and launched on the River Clyde, wonderful bone-shaking bicycles and colourful gypsy caravans, all telling the story of transport in Strathclyde.

Sir William Burrell (1861–1958)

William Burrell was a Glaswegian shipping merchant and a philanthropist. He began collecting works of art when he was still a teenager and during his lifetime he collected antiquities from all over the world, spending an average of £20,000 a year on his eclectic purchases. Burrell continued to collect after making his initial gift of over 9,000 items to the city in 1944, and a further 2,000 items were bequeathed after his death.

The Burrell Collection

The Burrell Collection

In the beautiful setting of Pollok Country Park, the Burrell Collection displays some of the thousands of items collected over a lifetime by Sir William Burrell. The collection was gifted to the City of Glasgow in 1944 with the condition that it be housed in a purpose-built gallery. There are 8,000 items, including stained glass and classical pieces, medieval tapestries and more than 600 great works of art. The park is easily accessed using public transport.

Pollok House

Pollok Country Park

Glasgow's largest park is just three miles south-west of the city centre. The ancestral home of the Maxwell family, the estate was gifted to the city in 1966. Take a woodland walk or enjoy the magnificent walled garden, the picnic areas and the children's activities. Pollok House, within the park, is a superb example of a William Adam house, with classical interiors and impressive formal gardens.

House for an Art Lover

House for an Art Lover

In 1901, Charles Rennie Mackintosh entered a competition set by a German magazine to design a house for an art lover. Mackintosh's dream to build the house became a reality some 90 years later when the building opened to the public in Bellahouston Park, three miles south-west of the city centre. The house includes a permanent exhibition of decoratively furnished rooms and the Art Lovers' Café and Shop. A programme of visual and musical events runs throughout the year.

Information

Visit Scotland Information Centre
11 George Square,
Glasgow G2 1DY
tel: 0845 22 55 121
email: info@visitscotland.com
website: www.visitscotland.com

Glasgow attractions

The Burrell Collection
0141 287 2550,
www.glasgowmuseums.com;
Fossil Grove
0141 950 1448,
www.glasgowmuseums.com;
Gallery of Modern Art
0141 287 3050,
www.glasgowmuseums.com;
Glasgow Botanic Gardens
0141 276 1614,
www.glasgow.gov.uk;
Glasgow Cathedral
0141 552 8198,
www.glasgowcathedral.org.uk;
Glasgow Police Museum
0141 552 1818,
www.policemuseum.org.uk;
Glasgow Royal Concert Hall
Box Office 0141 353 8000,
www.glasgowconcerthalls.
com/grch;
Glasgow Science Centre
0141 420 5000,
www.glasgowsciencecentre.org;
House for an Art Lover
0141 353 4770,
www.houseforanartlover.co.uk;
The Hunterian Museum and
Art Gallery
0141 330 4221 (museum)
0141 330 3618 (gallery)
www.hunterian.gla.ac.uk;

Hutchesons' Hall
0141 552 8391,
www.gnws.co.uk/glasgow/
museums/hutchesons_hall.htm;
Kelvingrove Art Gallery and
Museum
0141 276 9599,
www.glasgowmuseums.com;
Mackintosh House
0141 330 5431,
www.hunterian.gla.ac.uk/
collections/art_gallery/mac_
house/machouse_index.shtml;
People's Palace and Winter
Gardens
0141 276 0788,
www.glasgowmuseums.com;
Pollok House
0844 493 2202,
www.glasgowmuseums.com;
Provand's Lordship
0141 552 8819,
www.glasgowmuseums.com;
Ramshorn Theatre
0141 548 2542/0141 552 3489,
www.strath.ac.uk/culture/
ramshorn;
Riverside Museum Project
0141 287 2720,
www.glasgowmuseums.com;
Scotland Street School
Museum
0141 287 0500,
www.glasgowmuseums.com;
Scottish Exhibition &
Conference Centre
Box Office 0844 395 4000,
www.secc.co.uk;
Sharmanka Kinetic Gallery
0141 552 7080,
www.sharmanka.com;
St Mungo Museum of
Religious Life and Art
0141 276 1625,
www.glasgowmuseums.com;

The Tall Ship
0141 222 2513,
www.thetallship.com;
Tenement House
0844 493 2197,
www.nts.org.uk/Property/59;
Tron Theatre
Box Office 0141 552 4267,
www.tron.co.uk;
Willow Tea Rooms
0141 332 0521 (Sauchiehall
Street)/0141 204 5242
(Buchanan Street),
www.willowtearooms.co.uk

Tours and trips

Information on the following
tours and trips, and many
others, is available from the
Visit Scotland Information
Centre.

City Sightseeing Glasgow
0141 204 0444,
www.scotguide.com

Glasgow Taxis Guided Tours
0141 554 2222,
www.glasgowtaxisltd.co.uk/
services_tours.php

One-Day Mackintosh Trail
Ticket
Available from Visit Scotland
Information Centre, SPT
Travel Centres and all partici-
pating Mackintosh venues in
and around Glasgow or online
at www.crmsociety.com;
tel: 0141 946 6600

Scottish Tourist Guides
Association have a team of
Glasgow Guides
01786 451 953,
www.stga.co.uk

Index of attractions

World Pipe Band Championships

Contestants come from as far afield as Canada, the USA and the Middle East to compete at the annual World Pipe Band Championships held in Glasgow every August. The city centre resounds to the skirl of the pipes, and colourful bands in full highland dress parade through the streets to gather on Glasgow Green to compete. The championships have been associated with Glasgow since 1948 and there are contests for children as well as professional pipers.

Kibble Palace

Front cover main: Kelvingrove
Art Gallery & Museum; insets
l to r: 'Glasgow Rose', 'Heads',
Clyde Arc
Back cover: Glasgow Cathedral

Acknowledgements

Photography by Bob Lawson.
Additional photography by kind
permission of: Alamy: FCr, 2–3,16b,
20l, 21br (all David Robertson), FCc
& 18c (Nick Kirk), 17b (Yadid Levy),
21bl (Urbanmyth), 25r (Arcaid), 28b
(Mike Booth), 31l (Ian Cruickshank);
T & R Annan & Sons, Glasgow: 25l;
Bridgeman Art Library: 12r (Private
Collection), 19t (Glasgow City Council
Museums); Explore and Enjoy: 15tr
(inset); Mitchell Library: 11tr, 11b,
27br; Martin Moar: 11c, 24b; PCL
Travel: FC main; Photographers
Direct: FCl & 24t (Philip Game), 15tl
(Bronek Kaminski), 26r (Alex Ramsay);
seeglasgow.com: 5tl, 16t, 17t, 21t, 24c,
29 (all).

The publishers would like to thank
Anne Robertson of the Scottish Tourist
Guides Association, Visit Scotland
and the staff of various locations in
the guide for their assistance in its
preparation.

Written by Bob Lawson; the author
has asserted his moral rights.
Edited by Rachel Minay.
Designed by Nick Avery.
Additional picture research by Bob
Lawson and Rachel Minay.

Maps by The Map Studio, Romsey,
Hants, UK, based on Mapvu10
mapping produced by Lovell Johns
Ltd. Generated from Ordnance Survey
digital data with permission of The
Controller of Her Majesty's Stationery
Office © Crown Copyright. Licence
number 43368U.

Publication in this form © Pitkin
Publishing 2010.

Printed in Great Britain.
ISBN 978-1-84165-226-9   1/10

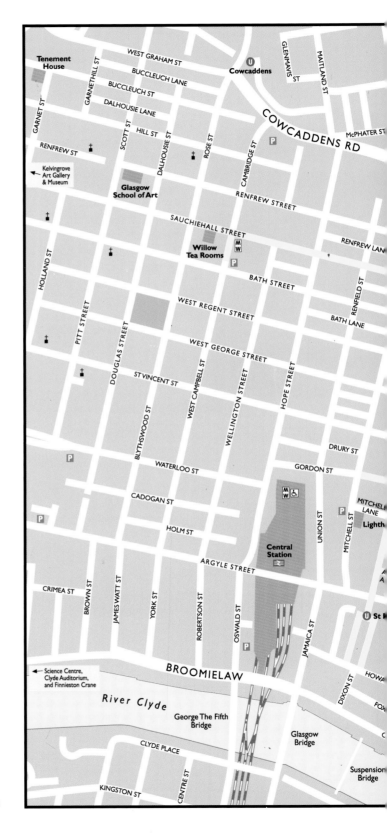